Eye Tricks

Sarah Fleming

Contents

What patterns can you see?

OXFORD
UNIVERSITY PRESS

(Damien Hurst)

Tricking your eyes

Sometimes what you see is not what you think you see. You look at something and see something different from what is there.

This picture looks as if the paper has gone wavy...

...and this one looks as if it curves. Can you make it curve out and then in?

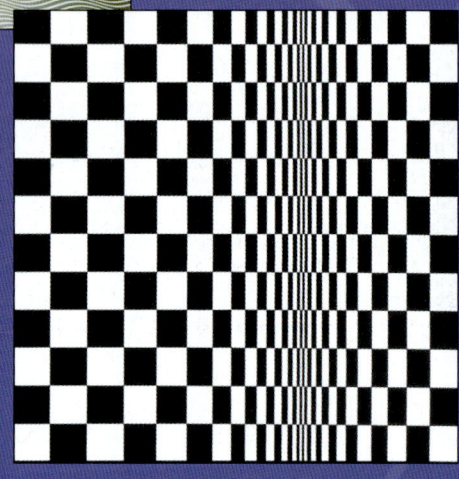

(Bridget Riley)

Lots of things can trick your eyes:

- the colour of something,
- where it is,
- what is around it,
- what you think you are going to see.

Making eye tricks

In this book there are instructions on how to make simple pictures that will trick the eye.

To make the eye tricks you will need:

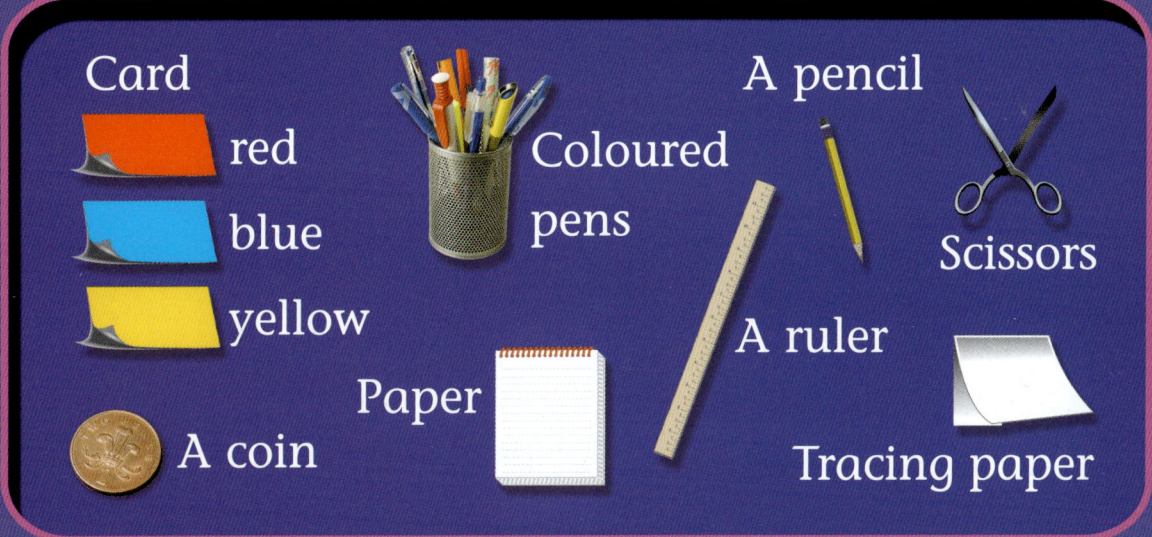

Card
red
blue
yellow
A coin
Paper
Coloured pens
A pencil
A ruler
Scissors
Tracing paper

Where you see this sign you can try to draw the trick on a computer. For some pictures, you will need to know how to Copy and Paste.

Colour tricks

Making the Trick

Use the scissors, the ruler and the card.

- Make four squares of card: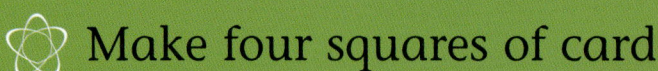

  - two red ones, 4 cm squared

  - one yellow one, 8 cm squared.

  - one blue one, 8 cm squared

- Put the big squares side by side. Put one red square in the middle of each of the big squares.

Doing the Trick

- Ask a friend which red square looks lighter.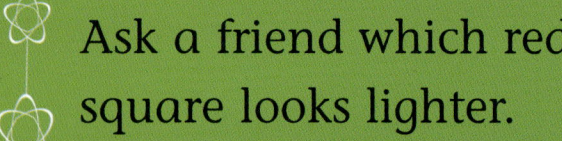

The red looks lighter or darker because of the different colours around it.

Here are some pictures where the colours look different because of the colours around them.

Can you see two different shades of red? In fact they are the same colour - it looks darker near the green.

The ring is a mid-grey colour.

If you split the picture in half, the two bits of the ring look as if they are two different greys.

If you slide one half of the picture down, the two bits of the ring look as if they are two different greys.

(Koffka ring)

Size tricks

Making the Trick

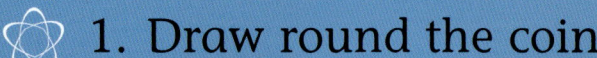 1. Draw round the coin.

Use the coin, some paper and the pencil.

2. Then, draw lots of small circles round it.

3. Draw round the coin again.

4. This time, draw a few, bigger circles round it.

Doing the Trick

Ask a friend which of the middle circles is bigger.

The size of the outer circles changes the way you see the middle one.

Here are pictures that trick our eyes because of what is close to them. Can you draw these on a computer?

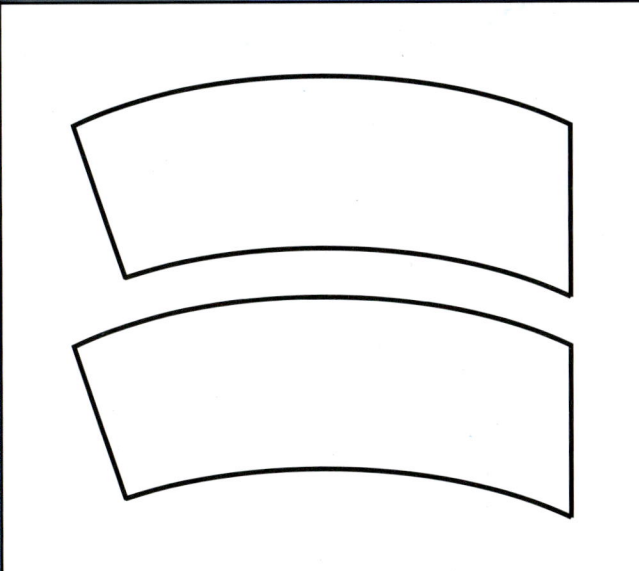

These curved shapes are the same size.

Which are bigger: the black squares or the white squares?

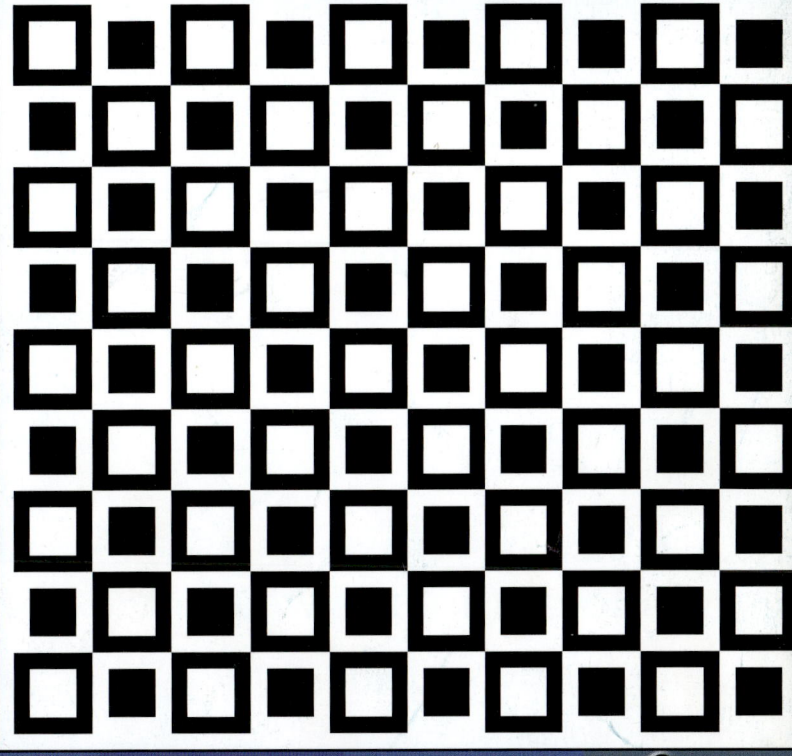

 # Brain tricks

Making the Trick

Use paper and coloured pens.

1. Use blue to write the word 'red.'

2. Write another colour word in a colour that is not the same as the colour word.

3. Cover your page with colour words like this.

Doing the Trick

Ask a friend to call out the colours (not the words) in the order on the page.

Part of the brain tries to say the colour, but another part of the brain tries to read the word. Which part wins?

 These pictures trick your eyes and your brain because what you read and what you see don't match up.

Is there a B or a 13 in the middle?

12
ABC
14

A
BIRD
IN THE
THE HAND

What is wrong with this phrase?

Tricks with parallel lines

Making the Trick

> Use paper, a pencil and a ruler.

1. Draw wide parallel lines diagonally across your paper.

2. Draw lots of short parallel lines across every other long line, like this.

3. Draw lots of short parallel lines up and down the other long lines, like this.

Doing the Trick

Ask a friend to find all the parallel lines.

> Most people can find the short parallel lines, but cannot see that the long lines are parallel.

In these pictures it looks as if the parallel lines bend because of what is around them.

Use a ruler to check that the lines are parallel.

Parallel lines (say pa-ra-llel) are lines that are the same distance apart for their whole length.

Diagonal line – a line which slants across the page.

Impossible tricks

Use tracing paper and a pencil.

Making the Trick

 Look carefully at this picture.
Can you trace it?

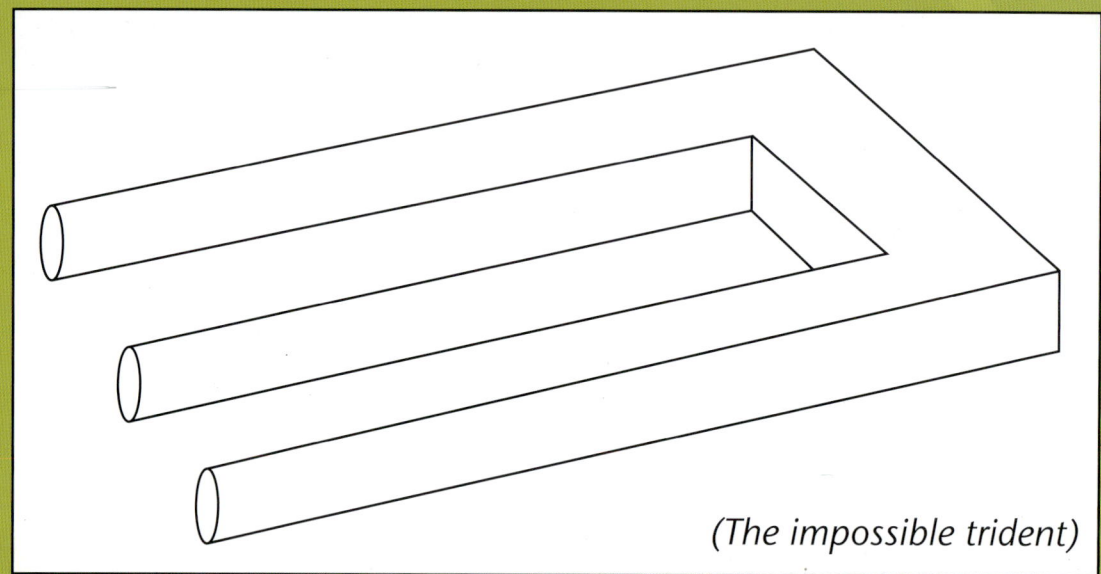

(The impossible trident)

Doing the Trick

 Ask a friend how many
prongs your picture has.

Why are these pictures impossible?

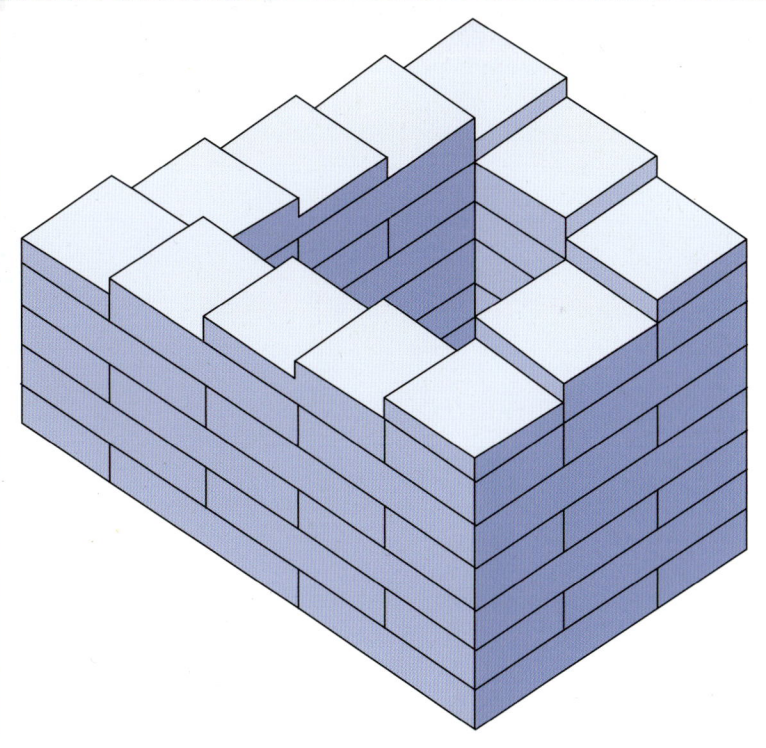

How many legs does this elephant have?

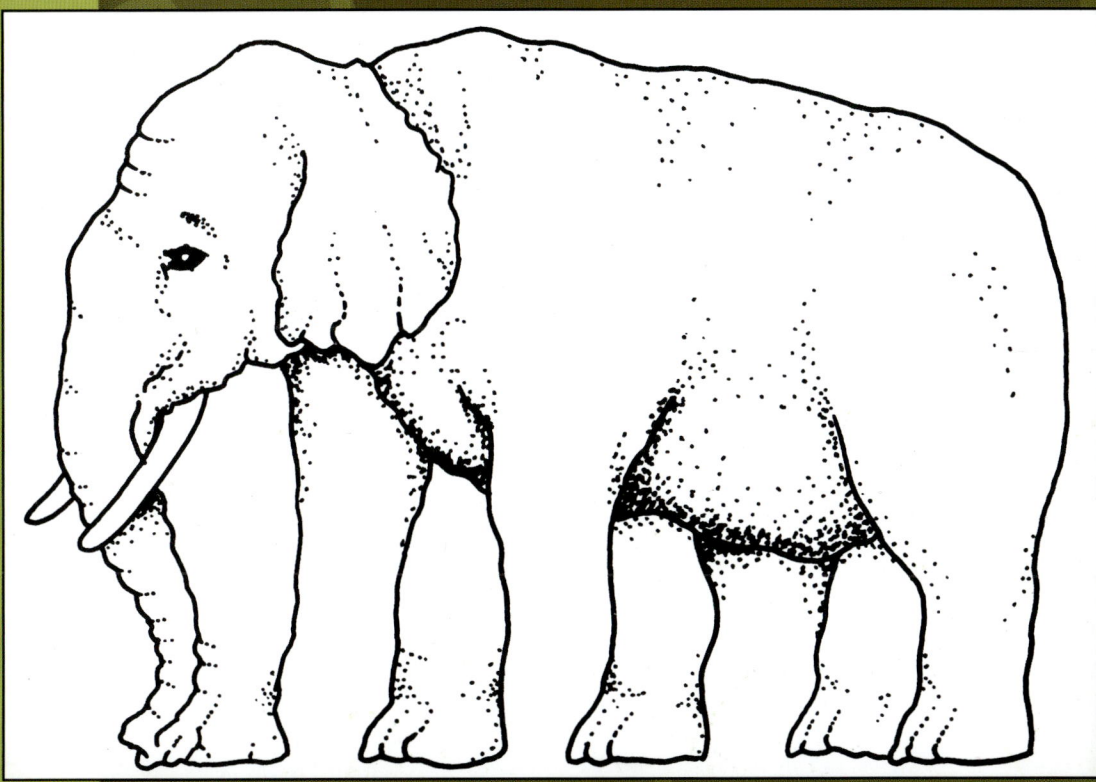

13

Finger trick

Doing the Trick

All you need are two hands and two eyes.

1. Hold your hands in front of you at eye level.

2. Point your index fingers at each other so that they touch.

3. Now look beyond your fingers at something further away.

4. Can you see a third finger floating between your two index fingers?

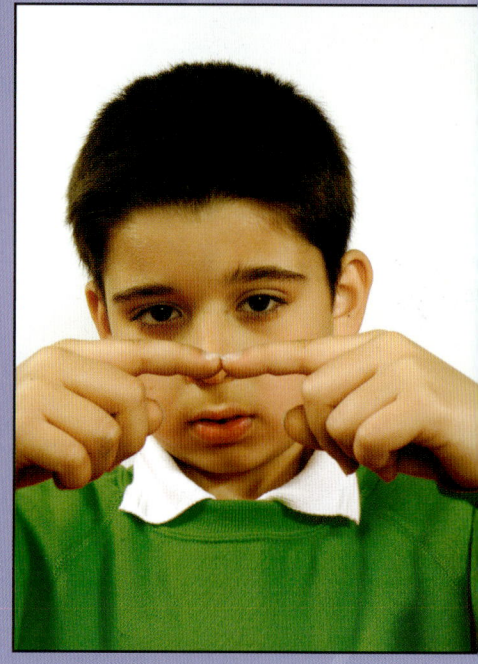

Move your index fingers apart a bit and see how short you can make your extra finger.

Look back

1   How can you make a coin look smaller?

2   What happens when you try to read a colour word that is written in a different colour?

3   Which page would you put this on. Why?

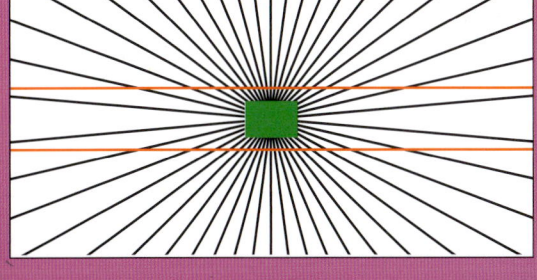

Index

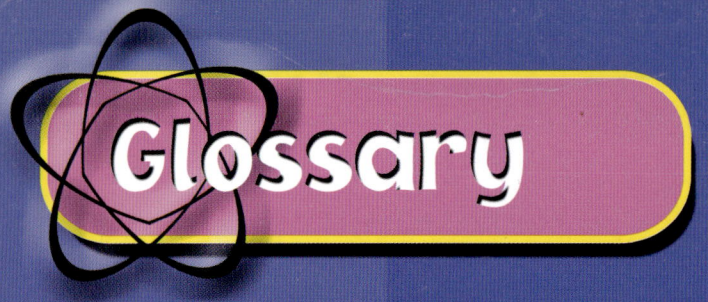

Glossary

brain The part of the body that lets you think and remember things. It also controls the body.

diagonal line A line which slants across the page.

impossible Something that cannot be done or cannot be real.

parallel lines Lines that are the same distance apart for their whole length.

prongs long, pointed ends e.g. of a fork, or a deer's antlers

trident A spear with three prongs.